1 | HERAKLION 2025

HERAKLION

Travel Guide

2025

Explore Crete's Rich History, Vibrant Culture, and Breathtaking Landscapes

ROBSON PHILLIP

All rights reserved. No part of this publication may be reproduced, distributed, or transmitted in any form or by any means, including photocopying, recording, or other electronic or mechanical methods, without the prior written permission of the publisher, except in the case of brief quotations embodied in critical reviews and certain other noncommercial uses permitted by copyright law.

Copyright © Robson Phillips, 2025.

Table of Contents

Introduction 7
   Why Visit Heraklion in 2025? 7
   Quick Facts and Overview 10

Planning Your Trip 18
   Best Times to Visit 18
   Travel Essentials 20
   Getting to Heraklion 22

Getting Around 27
   Public Transportation 27
   Taxis and Rideshares 29
   Car Rentals and Driving Tips 31

Top Attractions 35
   Knossos Palace: The Heart of Minoan Civilization 35
   Heraklion Archaeological Museum 37
   Koules Fortress 39
   Venetian Walls and Historic Gates 40
   Old Town and Lions Square 42

Cultural Experiences 45
   Festivals and Events 45
   Traditional Music and Dance 48
   Local Artisans and Handicrafts 50

Outdoor Adventures and Nature 54

- Hiking and Nature Trails 54
- Beaches: Matala, Ammoudara, and Beyond 57
- Boat Tours and Water Sports 60

Food and Drink 64
- Traditional Cretan Cuisine 64
- Best Restaurants and Taverns 67
- Wineries and Olive Oil Tours 69

Accommodations 74
- Luxury Resorts 74
- Boutique Hotels 76
- Budget-Friendly Stays 78
- Family-Friendly Options 80

Heraklion for Families 83
- Kid-Friendly Activities 83
- Parks and Playgrounds 86
- Educational Experiences 88

Day Trips from Heraklion 93
- Rethymno and Its Venetian Charm 93
- The Lassithi Plateau and the Cave of Zeus 96
- Elounda and Spinalonga Island 98
- Additional Recommendations 100

Go Shopping 102
- Souvenirs to Bring Home 102
- Local Markets and Boutiques 105

Modern Malls and Shopping Streets 109

Tips for Shopping in Heraklion 111

Practical Tips 113

Safety and Emergency Contacts 113

Language and Etiquette 116

Accessibility and Traveler Support 119

Sustainable Tourism 124

Eco-Friendly Activities in Heraklion 124

Responsible Travel Practices 131

Useful Resources 137

Maps 137

Recommended Apps for Travelers 139

Contact Information for Local Services 142

Conclusion 147

Making the Most of Your Heraklion Adventure 147

Final Travel Tips for Heraklion 148

INTRODUCTION

Heraklion, the vibrant capital of Crete, blends ancient wonders with modern energy, offering a perfect introduction to the island's rich history, culture, and Mediterranean charm. Known for its captivating archaeological treasures, bustling urban life, and stunning coastal scenery, Heraklion has something to enchant every traveler. Whether you're a history enthusiast, a foodie, a beach lover, or an adventure seeker, the city is a gateway to some of Crete's most fascinating experiences.

Why Visit Heraklion in 2025?

Heraklion's appeal is timeless, but visiting in 2024–2025 is particularly exciting due to new developments, anniversary celebrations, and increased accessibility. Here's why this period is an ideal time to explore the city:

1. Celebrating 3,000 Years of Minoan Heritage
2025 marks a significant anniversary of the Minoan civilization, with special events, exhibitions, and cultural festivals planned throughout the year. The legendary Palace of Knossos, just a short drive from the city, will host unique guided tours and multimedia experiences, bringing the stories of King Minos and the labyrinth of the Minotaur to life.

2. Enhanced Travel and Infrastructure: Heraklion International Airport, recently upgraded, ensures a smoother arrival experience for international and domestic visitors. With more direct flights from major cities and an improved ferry system, traveling to and from Heraklion has never been easier.

3. Sustainability Initiatives: Heraklion is embracing sustainable tourism with eco-friendly tours, plastic-free initiatives, and community-driven projects. Travelers can now enjoy green accommodations, farm-to-table dining, and activities that promote conservation and cultural preservation.

4. A Vibrant Cultural Scene: From music festivals and art exhibitions to traditional celebrations, Heraklion in 2024–2025 promises an exciting calendar of events. Don't miss the Cretan Wine Festival or the Kazantzakis Festival, which honors the legacy of the celebrated author of *Zorba the Greek*.

5. Perfect Year-Round Weather: Heraklion's Mediterranean climate ensures pleasant weather throughout the year. Whether you prefer warm summer days for beach outings or mild winters for sightseeing, the city welcomes you with open arms.

6. Affordable Luxury: Compared to other Mediterranean destinations, Heraklion offers excellent value for money. Visitors can indulge in luxurious experiences—from waterfront dining to five-star accommodations—without breaking the bank.

Quick Facts and Overview

To help you get acquainted with Heraklion, here are some quick facts about the city:

- **Location:** Central northern coast of Crete, overlooking the Aegean Sea.

- **Population:** Approximately 210,000, making it Crete's largest city and the fourth largest in Greece.

- **History:** Heraklion's history stretches back over 5,000 years, beginning as a Minoan settlement and evolving through Venetian, Ottoman, and modern Greek eras.

- **Language:** Greek is the official language, but English is widely spoken in tourist areas.

- **Currency:** Euro (€).

- **Time Zone:** Eastern European Time (EET), UTC+2.

- **Major Attractions:** Knossos Palace, Heraklion Archaeological Museum, Koules Fortress, Venetian Walls, and Lions Square.

- **Cuisine:** Known for its fresh seafood, olive oil, wine, and dishes like dakos, moussaka, and sfakianopita (honey cheese pie).

A Snapshot of Heraklion's History

Heraklion's rich history is inseparable from that of Crete itself. The Minoans, Europe's first advanced civilization, flourished here over 4,000 years ago. The archaeological site of Knossos, once the Minoan capital, stands as a testament to their architectural and artistic prowess.

Following the Minoan era, Heraklion saw waves of conquerors, each leaving their mark. The city thrived under Venetian rule (13th–17th centuries), evident in its formidable fortifications, elegant fountains, and basilicas. The Ottomans added their own influences, including mosques and public baths.

In the 20th century, Heraklion played a vital role in modern Greek history, enduring hardship during World War II and emerging as a dynamic cultural hub. Today, it bridges ancient and modern worlds, offering visitors a unique blend of historical depth and contemporary vibrancy.

What to Expect in Heraklion

Heraklion is not just a city to visit; it's a city to experience. Here's what makes it stand out:

1. A Gateway to the Past: History enthusiasts will find Heraklion a treasure trove of ancient artifacts, monuments, and stories. From exploring the ruins of Knossos to marveling at the exquisite frescoes and gold jewelry in the Archaeological Museum, every corner tells a tale of the past.

2. Bustling Urban Life: The city center is a hive of activity, with its bustling markets, lively squares, and vibrant café culture. Lions Square, with its iconic Morosini Fountain, serves as a central meeting point, surrounded by shops, restaurants, and landmarks.

3. Stunning Beaches: While Heraklion is more urban than other parts of Crete, it's still a fantastic base for beach lovers. Nearby stretches of golden sand, like Amoudara, Kokkini Hani, and Matala, offer pristine waters and a laid-back vibe.

4. A Culinary Haven: Heraklion's culinary scene is a highlight for many visitors. The city boasts a wide range of eateries, from traditional taverns serving hearty Cretan fare to upscale restaurants offering contemporary twists on local ingredients. Don't forget to pair your meals with a glass of raki or local wine.

5. Vibrant Nightlife: When the sun sets, Heraklion comes alive with bars, clubs, and music venues catering to all tastes. Whether you're in the mood for a quiet drink overlooking the harbor or a night of dancing, the city has you covered.

6. Proximity to Nature: Beyond the city limits, Heraklion offers access to some of Crete's most beautiful natural landscapes. Hike through rugged gorges, explore caves steeped in mythology, or take a scenic drive to traditional mountain villages.

Traveler Tips for Heraklion

To make the most of your visit, keep these tips in mind:

- **Stay Central:** Opt for accommodations near the city center or the harbor for easy access to attractions.

- **Time Your Visit:** Arrive early at popular sites like Knossos and the museum to avoid crowds.

- **Dress Comfortably:** Wear breathable fabrics and comfortable shoes, especially if you plan to explore archaeological sites or hike.

- **Learn a Few Phrases:** While English is widely spoken, knowing basic Greek greetings like *kalimera* (good morning) or *efharisto* (thank you) can go a long way.

- **Try the Local Specialties:** Don't leave without sampling dakos (Cretan rusk salad), kalitsounia (cheese pies), and loukoumades (Greek doughnuts).

Heraklion, with its rich history, lively atmosphere, and welcoming spirit, is more than just a travel destination—it's a journey into the heart of Crete. Whether you're uncovering the secrets of the

Minoans, savoring local delicacies, or soaking up the Mediterranean sun, Heraklion promises memories that will last a lifetime. As you plan your trip for 2024–2025, get ready to embark on an adventure that combines the best of Greece's past and present.

Planning Your Trip

Best Times to Visit

Heraklion, with its Mediterranean climate, offers something unique in every season. Here's a guide to help you choose the best time based on your interests:

- **Spring (March to May):** Perfect for mild weather, blooming landscapes, and fewer crowds. This is the ideal season for hiking, exploring archaeological sites, and enjoying festivals like Easter, celebrated with vibrant local traditions.

- **Summer (June to August):** Peak tourist season with hot, sunny days perfect for beachgoers and water sports enthusiasts. While popular attractions can get crowded, the lively

Travel Essentials

1. Visas

- **EU Citizens:** Travelers from the European Union and Schengen Area countries do not need a visa.

- **Non-EU Citizens:** Check visa requirements based on your country. Many nationalities, including the U.S., Canada, and Australia, can enter Greece visa-free for up to 90 days within a 180-day period.

- **Schengen Visa:** If required, apply for a Schengen visa through the Greek embassy or consulate in your country.

2. Currency

- Greece uses the **Euro (€)**.

atmosphere and extended daylight make it a fantastic time to visit.

- **Autumn (September to November):** A great time for wine tours, olive harvest festivals, and enjoying the warm sea. The weather is still pleasant, and the summer crowds have dispersed, making it a quieter and more affordable time to explore.

- **Winter (December to February):** Although cooler and wetter, winter offers a serene charm with fewer tourists. It's an excellent time for cultural experiences, visiting museums, and enjoying local cuisine in cozy taverns.

- ATMs are widely available, and major credit cards are accepted at most hotels, restaurants, and shops.

- For smaller establishments or rural areas, carrying cash is advisable.

3. Packing Tips

- **Clothing:**

  - Lightweight, breathable clothing for summer.

  - Layers and a light jacket for spring and autumn.

  - Warm clothes and waterproof gear for winter.

- **Footwear:** Comfortable walking shoes or sandals for city exploration and sturdy shoes for hiking.

- **Sun Protection:** Sunscreen, sunglasses, and a wide-brimmed hat are essential for sunny days.

- **Travel Adapters:** Greece uses Type C and F plugs, with a standard voltage of 230V.

Getting to Heraklion

Heraklion is well-connected to the rest of Greece and major international hubs, offering several convenient travel options:

1. Flights

- **Heraklion International Airport (HER):** The second-busiest airport in Greece, it offers flights from major European cities, including London, Berlin, and Paris, as well as domestic connections from Athens and Thessaloniki.

- **Direct Flights:** Seasonal charters and low-cost carriers provide direct flights from various global destinations during the summer.

Tips:

- ❖ Book flights early for the best deals, especially during peak seasons.

- ❖ The airport is a short 5 km (3 miles) from the city center, with taxis, buses, and car rentals readily available.

2. Ferries

- ❖ **From Athens (Piraeus Port):** Daily ferries connect Athens to Heraklion, with a journey time of 7–9 hours. Overnight ferries are a popular choice, offering cabins for a comfortable experience.

- **Inter-Crete Ferries:** Ferries also link Heraklion with other Cretan ports, such as Chania and Rethymno, as well as nearby islands like Santorini and Mykonos.

Tips:

- Check ferry schedules in advance, as they can vary by season.
- Opt for high-speed ferries for shorter travel times.

3. Road Options

- **Driving to Heraklion:** For those already on Crete, driving is a convenient way to reach Heraklion. The island's main highway, E75, connects the city to other major destinations.

- **Car Rentals:** Available at the airport and in the city, car rentals are ideal for exploring the region at your own pace.

- **Buses:**
The KTEL bus service operates reliable and affordable routes connecting Heraklion to other parts of Crete, including Chania, Rethymno, and Agios Nikolaos.

Tips:

- Drive cautiously, as some rural roads can be narrow or winding.

- Familiarize yourself with local driving laws and parking regulations.

With careful planning and these essential tips, your journey to Heraklion will be seamless and enjoyable. Whether you arrive by air, sea, or road, the city is ready to welcome you with its rich heritage, stunning landscapes, and warm hospitality.

Getting Around

Navigating Heraklion is straightforward, with various transportation options to suit different preferences and budgets. Whether you prefer public transit, taxis, or self-driving, here's everything you need to know:

Public Transportation

1. Buses

- **Overview:**

    Heraklion has an efficient and affordable bus network operated by KTEL, connecting the city center to suburbs, beaches, and nearby towns.

- **City Buses:** Frequent routes serve key areas like the port, airport, Knossos Palace, and Ammoudara beach.

- **Intercity Buses:** These connect Heraklion to other major cities in Crete, such as Chania, Rethymno, and Agios Nikolaos.

- **Fares:**

  Tickets can be purchased from kiosks, ticket offices, or directly from the driver (slightly higher price). Prices range from €1.50–€5.00 depending on the route.

- **Tips:**

  ➢ Check the bus schedule in advance, as services may be less frequent in the evening or offseason.

> Keep small change for tickets, as drivers may not always have change for large bills.

2. Airport Bus Service: Regular buses connect Heraklion International Airport to the city center, with a journey time of about 15–20 minutes. This is a cost-effective option for travelers arriving by air.

Taxis and Rideshares

1. Taxis

- **Availability:**
Taxis are widely available throughout Heraklion, especially in the city center, near major attractions, and at the airport.

- **Fares:**
Taxis operate on a metered system, with additional charges for luggage, nighttime travel, and airport pickups. Expect to pay

approximately €7–€10 for a short city ride and €15–€20 for trips to the airport.

- **How to Hail a Taxi:** You can flag down taxis on the street, find them at designated taxi ranks, or book in advance via phone or mobile apps.

2. Rideshares

- **Options:**

Rideshare services like Uber and Bolt are not yet widely available in Heraklion. However, local apps and taxi-booking platforms such as Taxiplon or Beat are popular alternatives.

- **Tips:**

  > Confirm the fare before starting your ride, especially for longer distances.

  > Tipping is not mandatory but appreciated (rounding up is common).

Car Rentals and Driving Tips

1. Renting a Car

- **Why Rent a Car?** Renting a car is an excellent option for exploring Heraklion's surrounding areas, such as Knossos Palace, mountain villages, and remote beaches.

- **Where to Rent:** Car rental agencies are abundant at the airport, city center, and online. International brands (Avis, Hertz) and local companies offer a range of vehicles.

- **Requirements:**

  - Valid driver's license (an International Driving Permit may be required for non-EU visitors).

  - Minimum age is usually 21, with a surcharge for drivers under 25.

- ❖ A credit card is typically needed for the security deposit.

- **Costs:**

Prices vary by season, with daily rates ranging from €30–€70 for a compact car.

2. Driving in Heraklion

- **Road Conditions:**

  - ❖ Roads in the city and main highways are generally well-maintained.

  - ❖ Rural roads can be narrow and winding, so drive cautiously.

- **Traffic:**

  - ❖ Traffic in the city center can be congested during peak hours.

- ❖ Parking is limited in busy areas; look for designated parking lots or opt for accommodations with parking facilities.

- **Fuel Stations:**

  - ❖ Gas stations are plentiful in the city and along major roads but may have limited hours in rural areas.

  - ❖ Most accept credit cards, though it's good to carry some cash as a backup.

- **Local Driving Laws:**

  - ❖ Drive on the right-hand side of the road.

  - ❖ Seat belts are mandatory for all passengers.

  - ❖ Using a mobile phone while driving is prohibited unless it's hands-free.

3. Tips for Exploring by Car

- Plan your routes in advance, as GPS signals can be spotty in mountainous regions.

- Always carry a copy of your rental agreement and insurance documents.

- Be respectful of local driving customs; Cretans are known for their relaxed, sometimes unpredictable driving style.

Working with these options and tips, getting around Heraklion will be easy and enjoyable, allowing you to focus on exploring the city's rich history, culture, and scenic beauty.

Top Attractions

Heraklion offers a fascinating blend of ancient history, Venetian architecture, and vibrant urban life. Here are the must-see attractions that make this city a cultural gem:

Knossos Palace: The Heart of Minoan Civilization

Overview:

The Palace of Knossos is one of the most iconic archaeological sites in Greece, located just 5 km south of Heraklion. It was the political and ceremonial center of the Minoan civilization, Europe's first advanced society, dating back over 3,000 years.

Highlights:

- **The Throne Room:** A beautifully preserved chamber featuring a stone throne and intricate frescoes.

- **The Queen's Megaron:** Famous for its Dolphin Fresco and advanced amenities, including one of the earliest known flushing toilets.

- **The Labyrinth Myth:** Legend has it that the palace housed the labyrinth where the Minotaur was imprisoned.

- **Restored Frescoes:** Vibrant depictions of Minoan life, including the famous "Prince of the Lilies."

Tips for Visitors:

- Visit early in the morning or late afternoon to avoid crowds and heat.

- Guided tours or audio guides are highly recommended for understanding the site's historical significance.

- Combine your visit with the Heraklion Archaeological Museum to see artifacts from Knossos.

Heraklion Archaeological Museum

Overview:

Located in the city center, this world-renowned museum is a treasure trove of artifacts from Crete's ancient past, including the Minoan, Roman, and Byzantine periods.

Highlights:

- **Phaistos Disc:** A mysterious clay disc with undeciphered symbols.

- **Bull-Leaping Fresco:** A vivid depiction of a Minoan ceremonial activity.

- **Minoan Jewelry:** Exquisite gold pieces showcasing the artistry of ancient Crete.

- **Linear A and B Tablets:** Early examples of written language in Europe.

Tips for Visitors:

- Allocate at least two hours to explore the museum's extensive collection.

- Consider purchasing a combined ticket for the museum and Knossos Palace.

- Photography is allowed, but flash is prohibited.

Koules Fortress

Overview:

Standing guard over the Venetian Harbor, Koules Fortress is a symbol of Heraklion's Venetian past. Built in the 16th century, it protected the city from invaders and served as a prison during the Ottoman era.

Highlights:

- **Defensive Architecture:** Massive stone walls, battlements, and inscriptions of the Venetian lion emblem.

- **Panoramic Views:** Stunning vistas of the harbor and city from the rooftop.

- **Exhibitions:** Displays of artifacts, models, and multimedia presentations about the fortress's history.

Tips for Visitors:

- The fortress is best visited during sunset for breathtaking views of the sea and skyline.

- Wear comfortable shoes, as the steps to the top can be steep.

- Don't miss the underground chambers, which provide a glimpse into its past as a prison.

Venetian Walls and Historic Gates

Overview:

The Venetian Walls encircle Heraklion's old town, a testament to the city's strategic importance during the Venetian era. These formidable fortifications, built in the 16th century, are among the best-preserved in Europe.

Highlights:

- **Martinengo Bastion:** The final resting place of Nikos Kazantzakis, the renowned author of *Zorba the Greek*.

- **Pantokrator Gate:** An impressive entry point adorned with Venetian reliefs.

- **Walking Path:** The walls provide a scenic route for walking, offering views of both the city and the sea.

Tips for Visitors:

- Walk along the walls early in the morning or late afternoon to avoid the heat.

- Visit the bastions for a deeper appreciation of the city's history.

- Guided tours are available for those interested in the military and architectural significance of the walls.

Old Town and Lions Square

Overview:

Heraklion's Old Town is a vibrant blend of history, culture, and modern life. At its heart lies Lions Square, the city's central meeting point, featuring the iconic Morosini Fountain.

Highlights:

- **Morosini Fountain:** A Venetian masterpiece adorned with intricately carved lions and mythological scenes.

- **25th of August Street:** A bustling pedestrian street lined with shops, cafés, and historic buildings.

- **Agios Titos Church:** A beautiful blend of Venetian and Byzantine architecture.

- **Local Markets:** The old town's markets, like the 1866 Street Market, offer a sensory delight of fresh produce, spices, and souvenirs.

Tips for Visitors:

- Explore the area on foot to fully appreciate its charm and hidden gems.

- Stop by a traditional café for a cup of Greek coffee or a slice of bougatsa (custard-filled pastry).

- Lions Square is perfect for people-watching, especially in the evening when the area comes alive.

Heraklion's top attractions showcase the city's diverse history, from its Minoan roots to its

Venetian and Ottoman influences. Whether you're exploring ancient ruins, strolling through historic streets, or admiring architectural marvels, Heraklion promises an unforgettable journey into Crete's cultural heart.

Cultural Experiences

Heraklion is not only rich in history but also alive with vibrant cultural traditions. Its festivals, music, and craftsmanship offer visitors a unique window into the heart of Crete's enduring heritage.

Festivals and Events

Heraklion's calendar is filled with lively festivals and events that celebrate its history, religion, and local traditions.

1. Carnival Season (Apokries):

- **When:** February/March (dates vary based on Easter).

- **What to Expect:** A colorful celebration leading up to Lent, featuring parades, masquerade parties, and traditional feasts. Families and visitors alike enjoy the festive atmosphere.

2. **Easter (Pascha):**

- **When:** Spring (date varies annually).

- **What to Expect:** Easter in Crete is a deeply spiritual and festive time. Witness solemn processions, candlelit midnight services, and the joyous breaking of the Lenten fast with traditional lamb dishes and tsoureki (sweet bread).

3. **Matala Beach Festival:**

- **When:** June.

- **What to Expect:** A music and art festival held in Matala, just south of Heraklion, celebrating the area's 1960s hippie history. Enjoy live performances, art exhibits, and workshops.

4. Wine and Harvest Festival:

- **When:** Late summer to early autumn.

- **What to Expect:** Celebrate Crete's winemaking traditions with tastings, music, dancing, and cultural events. Many local villages host their own smaller festivals during the grape harvest season.

5. Kazantzakis Festival:

- **When:** October.

- **What to Expect:** A tribute to Nikos Kazantzakis, Crete's most famous author, with literary events, readings, and cultural performances.

Traditional Music and Dance

Music and dance are integral to Cretan culture, expressing the island's history and spirit.

1. Cretan Lyra and Mandolin Music:

- The lyra, a three-stringed bowed instrument, is the soul of Cretan music, often accompanied by the mandolin.

- Songs tell stories of love, loss, and resilience, echoing Crete's history.

2. Traditional Dances:

- **Pentozali:** A lively war dance symbolizing bravery, performed at festivals and celebrations.

- **Syrtos:** A slower, more graceful dance, often performed in pairs or groups.

- **Maleviziotikos:** A high-energy dance featuring intricate footwork, showcasing the dancer's skill.

Where to Experience:

- Local festivals and weddings often feature live music and dance performances.

- Taverns and cultural venues in Heraklion occasionally host traditional music nights.

Tips for Visitors:

- Join in the dancing if invited—Cretans are known for their hospitality and love sharing their culture.

- Purchase CDs or digital recordings of Cretan music as a memorable souvenir.

Local Artisans and Handicrafts

Heraklion is home to skilled artisans who keep traditional crafts alive, blending centuries-old techniques with modern creativity.

1. Pottery:

- Crete's pottery tradition dates back to the Minoan era. Many workshops around Heraklion produce handmade ceramics, including vases, plates, and decorative pieces.

- **Where to Buy:** Visit the village of Thrapsano, known as the "potters' village," or explore artisan shops in Heraklion's old town.

2. Weaving and Textiles:

- Handwoven rugs, tapestries, and table linens reflect the intricate patterns and vibrant colors of Crete's cultural heritage.

- **Where to Buy:** Villages like Anogeia and smaller markets in Heraklion offer unique finds.

3. Knife Crafting:

- Traditional Cretan knives, often engraved with local proverbs, are both practical tools and symbolic gifts.

- **Where to Buy:** Specialty shops in Heraklion and workshops in rural villages.

4. Jewelry:

- Cretan jewelers craft exquisite pieces inspired by ancient Minoan designs, including gold pendants, rings, and bracelets.

- **Where to Buy:** Boutiques in Heraklion's shopping district or museum gift shops.

5. Raki and Olive Oil Production:

- Raki (a local spirit) and olive oil are essential to Cretan culture. Many family-owned producers offer tours, tastings, and products for purchase.

- **Where to Experience:** Visit olive mills or raki distilleries in nearby villages for a firsthand look at production processes.

Tips for Enjoying Heraklion's Culture

- **Be Curious:** Ask questions and show interest in local traditions; Cretans are eager to share their heritage.

- **Participate:** Whether it's learning a dance step, playing a lyra, or crafting pottery, hands-on experiences make lasting memories.

- **Take Home a Piece of Crete:** Handmade items, music, and local food products make meaningful souvenirs that support the island's artisans.

Heraklion's rich cultural tapestry offers countless ways to immerse yourself in the essence of Crete, ensuring an unforgettable journey.

Outdoor Adventures and Nature

Heraklion's stunning landscapes, from rugged mountains to pristine beaches, make it a paradise for outdoor enthusiasts. Whether you're an avid hiker, a beach lover, or an adventure seeker, there's no shortage of activities to immerse yourself in nature.

Hiking and Nature Trails

Heraklion's diverse terrain offers hiking experiences for all skill levels, ranging from leisurely walks to challenging treks.

1. Samaria Gorge (Day Trip):

- **Overview:** While not in Heraklion itself, the Samaria Gorge in western Crete is a must-visit for avid hikers. It's Europe's longest gorge at 16 km and features breathtaking cliffs, rare flora, and the chance to spot kri-kri (wild goats).

- **Tips:**
  - Wear sturdy hiking shoes and pack plenty of water.
  - Early morning starts are ideal to avoid crowds and heat.

2. Knossos to Archanes Trail:

- **Overview:** A scenic route starting at Knossos Palace and leading to the traditional village of Archanes. This trail combines history, nature, and local culture.

- **Highlights:** Lush vineyards, olive groves, and views of Mount Juktas, believed to be the burial place of Zeus.

3. Rouvas Gorge:

- **Overview:** Located near Zaros, this moderate-to-challenging trail offers dramatic canyon views, waterfalls, and a picnic area at the gorge's end.

- **Tips:**
    - Suitable for families with older children.
    - Spring and autumn are the best times to visit for comfortable weather.

4. Psiloritis (Mount Ida):

- **Overview:** The highest peak in Crete, Psiloritis offers a challenging but rewarding hike with panoramic views and the mythological Cave of Zeus along the way.

- **Tips:**

  ❖ Guided tours are recommended for less experienced hikers.

Beaches: Matala, Ammoudara, and Beyond

Heraklion's coastline is dotted with idyllic beaches, each offering a unique vibe and natural beauty.

1. Matala Beach:

- **Overview:** Famous for its sandstone caves and hippie culture of the 1960s, Matala is a laid-back spot ideal for swimming and snorkeling.

- **Highlights:**

  ❖ Crystal-clear waters.

- ❖ The iconic caves carved into the cliffs, once used as homes by ancient Romans and modern-day bohemians.

- ❖ Annual Matala Beach Festival with live music and art.

- **Tips:** Arrive early to secure a good spot, as this beach is popular.

2. Ammoudara Beach:

- **Overview:** A long, sandy beach just 5 km west of Heraklion. It's perfect for families and those looking for convenience and amenities.

- **Highlights:**

  - ❖ Watersports, including windsurfing and paddleboarding.

  - ❖ Lively beach bars and restaurants.

- ❖ Shallow waters, making it ideal for kids.

3. Agia Pelagia Beach:

- **Overview:** A picturesque bay with calm, turquoise waters surrounded by lush hills.

- **Highlights:**
  - ➢ Great for snorkeling and scuba diving.
  - ➢ Boutique hotels and taverns offering fresh seafood.

- **Tips:** Best visited during weekdays to avoid weekend crowds.

4. Komos Beach:

- **Overview:** A quieter alternative to Matala, Komos is a serene stretch of sand known for its unspoiled beauty.

- **Highlights:**

  ❖ Nesting site for loggerhead sea turtles (protected area).

  ❖ Sunset views over the Libyan Sea.

Boat Tours and Water Sports

The sea around Heraklion offers opportunities for adventure and exploration, whether you prefer relaxing boat rides or adrenaline-pumping activities.

1. Boat Tours to Nearby Islands:

- **Santorini Day Trips:** High-speed ferries and catamarans offer day trips to Santorini, where you can marvel at the caldera and iconic white-washed buildings.

- **Dia Island:** Just a short boat ride from Heraklion, this uninhabited island is perfect for snorkeling, diving, and enjoying secluded beaches.

2. Snorkeling and Scuba Diving:

- **Overview:** Heraklion's waters are teeming with marine life and underwater caves. Diving centers offer excursions for beginners and advanced divers.

- **Popular Spots:** Agia Pelagia and Dia Island.

3. Watersports:

- **Activities:** Jet skiing, windsurfing, paddleboarding, and parasailing are popular along Ammoudara Beach and other coastal spots.

- **Tips:**

- ❖ Book in advance during the summer season.
- ❖ Safety equipment is usually provided, but confirm with your operator.

4. Fishing Excursions:

- **Overview:** Local fishermen offer authentic fishing tours, giving you a chance to learn traditional techniques and enjoy a freshly caught meal.

Tips for Outdoor Adventures

- **Timing Matters:** Early mornings and late afternoons are best for outdoor activities, especially during the summer, to avoid the heat.
- **Stay Hydrated:** Always carry water and sun protection, as Heraklion can get very sunny.

- **Respect Nature:** Stick to designated trails, avoid disturbing wildlife, and leave no trace behind.

Heraklion's natural beauty provides endless opportunities to explore and connect with the outdoors, promising unforgettable adventures for all types of travelers.

Food and Drink

Heraklion's culinary scene is a feast for the senses, offering a blend of traditional Cretan flavors, locally sourced ingredients, and innovative dining experiences. From rustic taverns to modern restaurants and local wineries, the city is a gastronomic paradise.

Traditional Cretan Cuisine

Cretan cuisine is rooted in simplicity, freshness, and the Mediterranean diet. The island's fertile soil and mild climate provide an abundance of ingredients that define its distinctive dishes.

1. Must-Try Dishes:

- **Dakos:** A traditional appetizer of barley rusks topped with diced tomatoes, crumbled feta or mizithra cheese, olive oil, and oregano.

- **Kalitsounia:** Sweet or savory pastries filled with cheese or greens, often served as a snack or dessert.

- **Gamopilafo:** A rich rice dish traditionally served at weddings, cooked in goat or lamb broth and served with lemon.

- **Cretan Snails (Hohli Bourbouristi):** Snails sautéed in olive oil and rosemary, a local delicacy.

- **Apaki:** Smoked pork marinated in vinegar and herbs, perfect as a meze.

- **Sfakian Pie:** A thin cheese pie drizzled with honey, combining savory and sweet flavors.

- **Lamb with Stamnagathi:** Tender lamb cooked with wild greens, a perfect representation of Crete's farm-to-table tradition.

2. Local Staples:

- **Cretan Olive Oil:** Renowned for its quality, olive oil is a cornerstone of every meal.

- **Cheeses:** Graviera, anthotyros, and mizithra are popular local varieties.

- **Herbs and Greens:** Fennel, thyme, and wild greens are used extensively in cooking.

3. Desserts:

- **Loukoumades:** Fried dough balls drizzled with honey and cinnamon.

- **Kalitsounia (Sweet Version):** Filled with soft cheese and topped with powdered sugar or honey.

- **Rakomelo:** A sweet liqueur made from raki and honey, often served warm as a digestif.

Best Restaurants and Taverns

Heraklion offers a mix of traditional taverns, chic bistros, and seaside dining experiences. Here are some top recommendations:

1. Peskesi:

- **Overview:** A highly-rated restaurant that serves authentic Cretan dishes made with organic, locally sourced ingredients.

- **Highlights:** Dakos, lamb cooked in a clay pot, and traditional desserts.

2. Erganos:

- **Overview:** A family-run tavern that serves hearty portions of traditional Cretan fare in a cozy atmosphere.

- **Highlights:** Gamopilafo and staka (thickened butter) with eggs.

3. Kritamon:

- **Overview:** Located in the nearby village of Archanes, Kritamon offers an elevated dining experience with a focus on traditional recipes.

- **Highlights:** Creative takes on lamb and wild greens dishes.

4. Kouzeineri:

- **Overview:** A stylish eatery in the city center blending modern Mediterranean cuisine with Cretan influences.

- **Highlights:** Seafood dishes and innovative appetizers.

5. To Paradosiako:

- **Overview:** A hidden gem serving authentic home-cooked meals.

- **Highlights:** Try their moussaka and slow-cooked lamb.

6. Waterfront Restaurants:

- **Options:** Taverns along the Venetian Harbor serve fresh seafood and provide stunning views, particularly during sunset.

Wineries and Olive Oil Tours

Heraklion is at the heart of Crete's wine country, and its olive oil is world-renowned. Exploring these local treasures offers an immersive cultural and culinary experience.

1. Wineries to Visit:

- **Douloufakis Winery:**

  - Located in Dafnes, this family-run winery specializes in indigenous grape varieties like Vidiano and Liatiko.

  - **Experience:** Tours and tastings of award-winning wines.

- **Lyrarakis Winery:**

  - Situated in the village of Alagni, Lyrarakis is known for reviving rare Cretan grape varieties.

  - **Experience:** Scenic vineyard tours and wine-pairing sessions.

- **Boutari Winery:**

  ❖ A prestigious name in Greek wine, Boutari offers guided tours and tastings in its Heraklion vineyard.

  ❖ **Highlights:** Their signature red wines and barrel-aged whites.

2. Olive Oil Tours:

- **Cretan Olive Oil Farm:**

  ❖ Located near Agios Nikolaos, this farm offers insights into traditional olive oil production.

  ❖ **Experience:** Hands-on activities like harvesting and tasting sessions.

Koronekes Olive Mill:

- ❖ A family-owned mill where you can learn about cold-pressing techniques and sample premium olive oils.

3. Tips for Visitors:

- Combine a wine tour with a visit to nearby archaeological sites like Knossos for a full-day experience.

- Purchase small bottles of olive oil and wine as unique gifts or souvenirs.

- Most wineries and olive oil producers require reservations for tours, especially during peak seasons.

Heraklion's gastronomy is a celebration of Crete's rich heritage, natural bounty, and culinary artistry. Whether indulging in traditional dishes, savoring local wines, or exploring olive oil production, every meal becomes an unforgettable experience. Prepare your taste buds for a journey as memorable as the island itself!

Accommodations

Heraklion offers a wide range of accommodations to suit all preferences and budgets. From luxury resorts and boutique hotels to budget-friendly options and family-friendly stays, you'll find the perfect place to rest after exploring Crete's wonders.

Luxury Resorts

If you're looking for a lavish stay, Heraklion's luxury resorts provide top-notch amenities, stunning locations, and unparalleled service.

1. Blue Palace Elounda (Day Trip Distance):

- **Overview:** Located near Heraklion, this beachfront resort offers breathtaking views of Spinalonga Island.

- **Amenities:** Private infinity pools, fine dining restaurants, a world-class spa, and water sports.

- **Perfect For:** Couples seeking a romantic getaway or travelers who prioritize luxury and relaxation.

2. **Stella Island Luxury Resort & Spa:**

- **Overview:** An adults-only resort featuring overwater bungalows and an elegant, serene ambiance.

- **Amenities:** Lagoon-style pools, gourmet dining, and personalized spa treatments.

- **Perfect For:** Honeymooners or those celebrating special occasions.

3. Capsis Astoria Heraklion:

- **Overview:** A sophisticated hotel in the heart of Heraklion city, blending modern comfort with classic elegance.

- **Amenities:** Rooftop pool and bar, fine dining, and easy access to key attractions.

- **Perfect For:** Travelers who want luxury with a convenient city-center location.

Boutique Hotels

Boutique hotels in Heraklion provide unique charm, personalized service, and intimate settings.

1. Lato Boutique Hotel:

- **Overview:** A stylish hotel near the Venetian Harbor, offering contemporary rooms and suites with harbor views.

- **Highlights:** Rooftop dining at Herbs' Garden restaurant and proximity to cultural landmarks.

- **Perfect For:** Couples or solo travelers seeking a chic yet affordable stay.

2. Olive Green Hotel:

- **Overview:** An eco-friendly boutique hotel that combines sustainability with modern design.

- **Highlights:** Smart room technology, locally sourced breakfast options, and a focus on green initiatives.

- **Perfect For:** Environmentally conscious travelers.

3. GDM Megaron Hotel:

- **Overview:** A historic building transformed into a luxury boutique hotel in the city center.

- **Highlights:** Rooftop pool, gourmet restaurant, and proximity to the Archaeological Museum.

- **Perfect For:** History buffs and those who appreciate refined elegance.

Budget-Friendly Stays

Travelers on a budget can still find comfortable and clean accommodations in Heraklion without sacrificing convenience.

1. Kronos Hotel:

- **Overview:** A family-run hotel near the city center, offering basic yet cozy rooms.

- **Highlights:** Affordable rates, friendly service, and proximity to Lions Square.

- **Perfect For:** Backpackers and budget-conscious travelers.

2. Athinaiko Hotel:

- **Overview:** A simple, well-maintained hotel offering excellent value for money.

- **Highlights:** Free Wi-Fi, breakfast options, and walking distance to the bus station.

- **Perfect For:** Travelers looking for convenience and affordability.

3. Rea Hotel:

- **Overview:** A small, no-frills hotel in a central location.

- **Highlights:** Quiet rooms, helpful staff, and easy access to attractions.

- **Perfect For:** Solo travelers or those on a tight budget.

Family-Friendly Options

Families visiting Heraklion will find plenty of accommodations catering to children, with spacious rooms, kid-friendly amenities, and activities.

1. Fodele Beach & Water Park Resort:

- **Overview:** A family-oriented resort featuring a private beach and a water park.

- **Amenities:** Kids' clubs, multiple pools, and family-friendly dining options.

- **Perfect For:** Families with young children who want a mix of relaxation and entertainment.

2. Galaxy Hotel Iraklio:

- **Overview:** A modern hotel in the city center with family suites and excellent facilities.

- **Amenities:** Outdoor pool, kids' menu, and babysitting services.

- **Perfect For:** Families seeking city convenience with luxurious touches.

3. Apollonia Beach Resort & Spa:

- **Overview:** A beachfront resort offering plenty of activities for kids and adults alike.

- **Amenities:** Playgrounds, a mini club, and organized excursions.

- **Perfect For:** Multi-generational families or groups.

Tips for Choosing Accommodations

- **Book Early:** Heraklion is a popular destination, especially in the summer, so secure your stay in advance.

- **Consider Location:** Choose accommodations based on your planned activities. City hotels are ideal for cultural exploration, while beachfront resorts are great for relaxation.

- **Look for Packages:** Many resorts and hotels offer special deals, including meal plans, excursions, or spa packages.

Heraklion's wide range of accommodations ensures that every traveler can find a perfect home away from home, whether you're seeking luxury, charm, affordability, or family-friendly amenities.

Heraklion for Families

Heraklion is a fantastic destination for families, offering activities and attractions that cater to all ages. Whether your kids are adventurers, history enthusiasts, or nature lovers, the city provides endless opportunities for fun and learning.

Kid-Friendly Activities

1. Cretaquarium (Thalassocosmos):

- **Overview:** One of the largest aquariums in Europe, showcasing a diverse range of marine life from the Mediterranean Sea.

- **Highlights:**
  - Shark tanks, jellyfish exhibits, and interactive touch pools.

- ❖ Educational programs and activities designed for children.

- **Tips:** Allocate at least 2–3 hours and bring a camera for capturing moments with sea creatures.

2. Dinosauria Park:

- **Overview:** An interactive park featuring life-size dinosaur models and activities that teach kids about prehistoric life.

- **Highlights:**
  - ❖ Excavation areas where kids can dig for "fossils."
  - ❖ A 5D cinema experience that brings dinosaurs to life.

- **Perfect For:** Young paleontology enthusiasts.

3. Watercity Water Park:

- **Overview:** A fun-filled water park located just outside Heraklion.

- **Highlights:**
  - Water slides, lazy rivers, and kid-friendly pools.
  - On-site restaurants and shaded areas for family relaxation.

- **Tips:** Arrive early to avoid long lines and pack sunscreen and swimwear.

4. Beach Days:

- **Best Options:**
  - **Ammoudara Beach:** Shallow waters and amenities make it ideal for families.

- **Matala Beach:** Famous for its caves, which kids will love exploring.

- **Agia Pelagia:** Calm waters perfect for swimming and snorkeling with little ones.

5. Horse Riding:

- **Overview:** Local farms and stables offer family-friendly horse-riding experiences through the Cretan countryside.

- **Tips:** Check with operators for child-friendly sessions and safety gear.

Parks and Playgrounds

1. Georgiadis Park:

- **Overview:** A large green space in the heart of Heraklion, offering a tranquil escape for families.

- **Highlights:**
  - ❖ Playgrounds with swings, slides, and climbing structures.
  - ❖ Cafés and snack kiosks for parents to relax.
- **Tips:** Bring a picnic or snacks to enjoy under the shade of the trees.

2. Knossos Archaeological Site:

- **Overview:** While primarily a historical attraction, Knossos offers open spaces and intriguing ruins that kids can explore.
- **Tips:** Engage children with stories of Greek mythology to make the visit more exciting.

3. Mount Youchtas Nature Park:

- **Overview:** A nature reserve offering hiking trails, picnic areas, and plenty of opportunities to spot wildlife.

- **Perfect For:** Families who enjoy outdoor adventures and nature walks.

4. Local Playgrounds:

- Many neighborhoods in Heraklion have small, well-maintained playgrounds where kids can burn off energy.

Educational Experiences

1. Heraklion Archaeological Museum:

- **Overview:** One of Greece's most significant museums, home to artifacts from the Minoan civilization.

- **Family Highlights:**

- ❖ Interactive exhibits and child-friendly explanations of ancient history.

- ❖ Workshops designed for kids to engage with the past creatively.

- **Tips:** Opt for a guided tour or family activity pack to make the visit more engaging for children.

2. Natural History Museum of Crete:

- **Overview:** A hands-on museum featuring exhibits about Crete's flora, fauna, and geology.

- **Highlights:**

  - ➢ Earthquake simulator and life-sized animal models.

  - ➢ Fun, interactive activities that make learning exciting.

3. Kazantzakis Museum:

- **Overview:** Dedicated to the life and works of Nikos Kazantzakis, one of Greece's most famous authors.

- **Perfect For:** Older kids interested in literature or Greek culture.

4. Olive Oil and Wine Tours:

- **Kid-Friendly Options:** Many tours include demonstrations of traditional olive pressing and grape harvesting, which can be fascinating for children.

5. Pottery and Art Workshops:

- **Overview:** Local artisans often host workshops where kids can learn to create traditional Cretan pottery or try painting.

- **Perfect For:** Sparking creativity and giving kids a unique souvenir to take home.

Tips for Families Visiting Heraklion

- **Plan Ahead:** Many attractions, especially outdoor ones, are best visited in the morning or late afternoon to avoid peak heat.

- **Pack Essentials:** Bring sunscreen, hats, and water bottles for your adventures.

- **Engage Kids with Stories:** Use myths, legends, and history to make sites like Knossos and the museum come alive for children.

- **Combine Fun with Learning:** Balance educational stops with playtime at beaches or parks.

Heraklion is a wonderful destination for families, offering a mix of fun, education, and relaxation that ensures everyone has a memorable vacation.

Day Trips from Heraklion

Heraklion's central location makes it an excellent base for exploring Crete's stunning landscapes, historical sites, and charming towns. These day trips offer a mix of cultural, natural, and historical experiences, making them perfect for travelers looking to delve deeper into the island's treasures.

Rethymno and Its Venetian Charm

Travel Time: ~1 hour by car or bus

Rethymno is a picturesque town on Crete's northern coast, known for its Venetian and

Ottoman influences, charming old town, and vibrant cultural scene.

Highlights:

1. **The Old Town:**

    ❖ Wander through narrow cobblestone streets lined with colorful houses, quaint cafés, and boutique shops.

    ❖ Explore Venetian-era mansions and admire the blend of Renaissance and Ottoman architecture.

2. **The Fortezza:**

    ❖ A well-preserved Venetian fortress overlooking the sea.

    ❖ Offers stunning views and a glimpse into the town's strategic history.

3. **Rimondi Fountain:**

    ❖ A beautiful Venetian-era fountain in the heart of the Old Town.

    ❖ A popular spot for photos and a refreshing pause during your stroll.

4. **Beaches:**

    ❖ Relax on Rethymno's long sandy beach, ideal for families and water sports enthusiasts.

Tips:

- Combine your visit with a meal at a seaside taverna. Try fresh seafood and local specialties like kalitsounia.

- Wear comfortable shoes for exploring the old town's cobblestone streets.

The Lassithi Plateau and the Cave of Zeus

Travel Time: ~1.5 hours by car

The Lassithi Plateau is a serene area surrounded by mountains, dotted with traditional villages and known for its windmills and mythological significance.

Highlights:

1. **The Cave of Zeus (Dikteon Cave):**

    - According to Greek mythology, this is the birthplace of Zeus, the king of the gods.

    - A short but slightly steep hike leads to the cave, where you can explore its impressive stalactites and stalagmites.

2. **Windmills of Lassithi:**

- Iconic white-sailed windmills that once dotted the plateau, some of which are restored and operational.

- A great spot for photos and learning about Crete's agricultural history.

3. **Traditional Villages:**

    - Visit villages like Tzermiado or Psychro for a glimpse of rural Cretan life.

    - Stop at a local café (kafeneio) to enjoy a cup of Greek coffee and homemade treats.

4. **Eco Park and Interactive Experiences:**

    - Participate in workshops on pottery, olive oil production, or bread baking, which are perfect for families.

Tips:

- Bring sturdy shoes for the cave hike and a jacket, as it can be cool inside.

- Start early to avoid crowds at the cave and enjoy a leisurely exploration of the plateau.

Elounda and Spinalonga Island

Travel Time: ~1 hour by car or bus to Elounda, followed by a short boat ride to Spinalonga

Elounda is a luxurious coastal town with beautiful beaches and crystal-clear waters, while Spinalonga Island offers a unique blend of history and beauty.

Highlights:

1. **Spinalonga Island:**

    ❖ A small island with a Venetian fortress and a poignant history as a leper colony.

- Explore the well-preserved fortifications, old buildings, and scenic views of the bay.

2. **Elounda:**

    - Relax on its pristine beaches or enjoy a swim in its calm, shallow waters.
    - Take a leisurely stroll along the waterfront, lined with tavernas and boutiques.

3. **Plaka Village:**

    - A charming fishing village near Elounda, offering stunning views of Spinalonga.
    - Ideal for a traditional seafood meal.

4. **Kolokytha Peninsula:**

    - A serene area near Elounda with hidden coves and walking trails, perfect for nature lovers.

Tips:

- Pack comfortable walking shoes for Spinalonga's uneven terrain.

- Consider a guided tour of Spinalonga to learn about its fascinating history.

- Combine your visit with a swim at Kolokytha Beach or a meal in Plaka.

Additional Recommendations

- **Pack Essentials:** Sunscreen, hats, and water bottles are crucial, especially for outdoor adventures.

- **Start Early:** Most destinations are less crowded in the morning, allowing for a more relaxed experience.

- **Transport Options:** While buses connect Heraklion to many destinations, renting a car offers more flexibility for exploring at your own pace.

Heraklion's proximity to these incredible locations ensures that your day trips will be as enriching and memorable as your time in the city.

Go Shopping

Heraklion offers a delightful shopping experience, blending traditional crafts, local products, and contemporary fashion. Whether you're looking for a unique souvenir, exploring bustling markets, or indulging in high-end shopping, Heraklion's diverse retail options cater to every style and budget.

Souvenirs to Bring Home

1. Cretan Olive Oil and Products:

- **What to Buy:** Extra virgin olive oil is the essence of Cretan cuisine, and many local producers offer high-quality bottles. You can also find olive oil-based soaps, lotions, and beauty products.

- **Where to Shop:** Local shops and markets, such as the Heraklion Central Market or specialized olive oil stores.

2. Cretan Wines and Spirits:

- **What to Buy:** Crete is known for its indigenous wine varieties such as Vidiano and Liatiko. Raki (Cretan spirits) is also a popular souvenir.

- **Where to Shop:** Wineries, local tavernas, and wine shops, especially in the Old Town.

3. Handmade Pottery:

- **What to Buy:** Traditional Cretan pottery, including decorative pieces, plates, and bowls. Look for distinctive designs inspired by the island's culture and nature.

- **Where to Shop:** Artisan shops in Heraklion, particularly those near the Venetian Harbor.

4. Cretan Cheese:

- **What to Buy:** Graviera, Mizithra, and Anthotyros are some of Crete's famous cheeses. Consider buying vacuum-sealed packs for easy transport.

- **Where to Shop:** Local dairies or specialty stores.

5. Handwoven Textiles:

- **What to Buy:** Cretan rugs, tablecloths, and scarves made from natural fibers like cotton and wool. These textiles feature traditional designs and vibrant colors.

- **Where to Shop:** Local craft shops and markets.

6. Cretan Herbal Products:

- **What to Buy:** Dried herbs such as oregano, thyme, and sage, as well as herbal teas and honey.

- **Where to Shop:** Markets and specialized herb shops.

Local Markets and Boutiques

1. Heraklion Central Market (Modiano Market):

- **Overview:** A lively, vibrant market located near Lions Square, selling fresh produce, meats, cheeses, spices, and Cretan specialties.

- **What to Find:**
  - Local olives, olive oil, cheeses, and honey.
  - Dried herbs and spices.
  - Traditional sweets like loukoumades and baklava.

- **Tips:** Wander the market and enjoy the sensory experience of bustling stalls. Be sure to try some samples!

2. 1866 Street:

- **Overview:** One of the main shopping streets in Heraklion, filled with boutiques and specialty stores.

- **What to Find:**

  - ❖ Fashion boutiques with stylish clothing and accessories.

  - ❖ Local jewelry, including designs inspired by Minoan culture.

  - ❖ Souvenirs such as handcrafted wooden items and leather goods.

3. Morosini Fountain Area:

- **Overview:** Surrounding the famous Morosini Fountain, this area is home to a variety of shops and cafes.

- **What to Find:**

  ❖ Souvenir shops with Cretan-inspired gifts and local art.

  ❖ Small art galleries showcasing contemporary and traditional Cretan works.

4. Old Town of Heraklion:

- **Overview:** The winding streets of Heraklion's Old Town are home to charming boutiques and artisan stores.

- **What to Find:**

  - Handmade leather goods, including sandals, belts, and bags.

  - Local art and pottery.

  - Traditional Greek jewelry with a modern twist.

5. Traditional Craft Shops:

- **Overview:** Heraklion is home to several shops offering handmade crafts and local art. These items often reflect the island's rich culture and traditions.

- **What to Find:**

  - Handmade wooden products, including toys and kitchen utensils.

  - Ceramics featuring ancient Cretan designs.

- Handmade textiles, including blankets and shawls.

Modern Malls and Shopping Streets

1. Talos Plaza Mall:

- **Overview:** One of the largest shopping centers in Heraklion, located near the harbor.

- **What to Find:**
  - International and Greek brands for fashion, accessories, and cosmetics.
  - Cafés, restaurants, and a cinema for a break from shopping.

- **Tips:** Ideal for those looking for a more conventional mall experience with modern amenities.

2. Hersonissos:

- **Overview:** Just a short drive from Heraklion, this lively coastal town offers a wide range of shopping options.

- **What to Find:**

  - Trendy boutiques and fashion stores.
  - Beachwear and summer essentials.
  - Souvenirs and hand-crafted jewelry.

3. The Mall of Heraklion (Lidl Mall):

- **Overview:** A shopping complex with a variety of stores selling clothes, accessories, and home goods. It's a great place for those looking for both international brands and local products.

- **What to Find:**

  - Affordable clothing and accessories.

- Sporting goods and household items.

4. 25th August Street:

- **Overview:** This bustling pedestrian street in Heraklion is a great place to find both local shops and international chains.

- **What to Find:**

    - Fashion stores, including Greek designers and European brands.
    - Jewelry, watches, and accessories.
    - Leather goods and small gift shops.

Tips for Shopping in Heraklion

- **Bargaining:** While bargaining is not common in most stores, it's always appreciated in local markets, especially for souvenirs.

- **Tax-Free Shopping:** Non-EU visitors can take advantage of tax-free shopping, where they can claim a refund for VAT on certain items.

- **Local Payment Methods:** Credit and debit cards are widely accepted, but it's always handy to have some cash for smaller purchases, especially at markets and small shops.

Whether you're looking for local products, trendy fashion, or unique gifts, Heraklion's shopping scene offers something for everyone. From traditional markets to modern malls, you'll be sure to find the perfect souvenir or treat yourself to something special.

Practical Tips

Heraklion is a safe and welcoming destination for travelers, offering rich cultural experiences and a variety of activities. To help you make the most of your trip, here are some essential practical tips for navigating the city.

Safety and Emergency Contacts

1. General Safety:

- **Overview:** Crete is generally considered a very safe destination for tourists. The locals are friendly and welcoming, and petty crime like pickpocketing is rare, especially in smaller towns and rural areas. However, like any tourist destination, it's important to stay alert, especially in crowded areas.

- **Travel Safety Tips:**

  ❖ Keep an eye on your belongings in busy tourist spots or markets.

  ❖ Use hotel safes to store valuables and documents.

  ❖ Be cautious when driving or walking in unfamiliar areas, particularly at night.

2. Emergency Contacts:

- **Police:** Dial 100 for police assistance in any emergency.

- **Ambulance:** Dial 166 for medical emergencies.

- **Fire Department:** Dial 199 for fire emergencies.

- **General Emergency Number:** In case of any emergency, dial 112, which is the European Union emergency number.

3. Healthcare Services:

- **Pharmacies:** Pharmacies are widely available in Heraklion, and many are open during business hours. Some pharmacies offer extended hours for emergencies, and the staff often speaks basic English.

- **Hospital:** The University General Hospital of Heraklion is the main hospital on the island. It's well-equipped and handles emergencies.

- **Travel Insurance:** It's highly recommended to have comprehensive travel insurance that covers health care, especially if you plan to engage in outdoor activities or water sports.

4. Avoiding Scams:

- **Taxis:** While taxis in Heraklion are generally trustworthy, always check that the meter is on or agree on a fare before starting your journey.

- **ATMs:** Use ATMs located in well-lit, busy areas. Be cautious of using ATMs in isolated locations.

Language and Etiquette

1. Language:

- **Official Language:** Greek is the official language of Crete. However, many people in Heraklion speak English, especially in tourist areas, restaurants, and hotels.

- **Useful Greek Phrases:**
    - **Hello/Goodbye:** Kalimera (Καλημέρα)
    - **Please:** Parakaló (Παρακαλώ)

- **Thank you:** Efharistó (Ευχαριστώ)

- **Yes/No:** Ne (Ναι) / Ochi (Όχι)

- **How much is this?:** Poso kani afto? (Πόσο κάνει αυτό;)

- **Tips for Communication:** While most locals can communicate in English, learning a few basic Greek phrases will be appreciated and add to your cultural experience.

2. Etiquette:

- **Politeness:** Greeks value politeness, so a warm greeting with a friendly smile is always appreciated. Addressing people with respect and using "please" and "thank you" will go a long way.

- **Tipping:** Tipping is not obligatory but is always appreciated. In restaurants, a 5-10% tip is common if service is not included. Small tips for taxi drivers and hotel staff are also customary.

- **Dress Code:** In general, dress is casual for tourists. However, when visiting churches or monasteries, it's respectful to dress modestly (cover shoulders and knees).

- **Photography Etiquette:** Ask for permission before photographing people, especially in rural or local settings. It's also courteous to be mindful of local customs and traditions, particularly in religious sites.

3. Eating Etiquette:

- **Dining Times:** Lunch in Crete is typically served between 1:00 pm and 3:00 pm, while dinner is usually after 8:00 pm. Many restaurants open later in the evening, so be prepared for a late dinner.

- **Sharing Meals:** Cretans often enjoy meals family-style, with a variety of dishes shared among the table. If invited to a local's home, expect to share food, and don't refuse the offer.

- **Wine and Raki:** If offered a glass of raki (Cretan spirit), it is customary to accept. It's seen as a gesture of hospitality.

Accessibility and Traveler Support

1. Public Transportation Accessibility:

- **Buses:** The public bus system in Heraklion is quite reliable and affordable. Most buses are accessible to travelers with limited mobility, but check in advance if you require special accommodations.

- **Taxis and Rideshares:** Taxis are easily available in Heraklion, and most drivers are helpful. If you need a wheelchair-accessible taxi, it's best to arrange one in advance through your hotel or a local taxi service. Rideshare apps like Bolt are also popular in the city.

2. Wheelchair Access and Disabled Services:

- **Accommodation:** Many hotels in Heraklion offer wheelchair-friendly rooms and accessible entrances, but it's advisable to check accessibility details with your accommodation beforehand.

- **Public Restrooms and Attractions:** While many of Heraklion's public spaces are becoming more accessible, some older buildings and historical sites may lack wheelchair-friendly facilities.

- **Assistance Services:** If you have mobility issues, you may want to arrange for assistance at major transportation hubs (such as the airport or ferry terminal) in advance.

3. Information and Traveler Support:

- **Tourist Information Centers:** There are several tourist information points in Heraklion, including one at the Heraklion Port and another near Lions Square. They provide brochures, maps, and helpful advice about the city and surrounding areas.

- **Visitor Services:** Hotels and many attractions provide information in English, and staff are generally helpful to international visitors. For any issues, the local tourism office is a good point of contact.

- **Emergency Help for Travelers:** In case of emergencies, most of the tourist areas, including the Old Town, have English-speaking staff available. You can also reach out to your embassy or consulate for additional support.

Final Tips for a Smooth Trip to Heraklion:

- **Cash and Cards:** While credit cards are widely accepted, it's still a good idea to carry cash, especially for small purchases or at more traditional establishments.

- **Weather Considerations:** The summer months (June to August) can be very hot, so pack light clothing, sunscreen, and a hat. In winter (December to February), the weather is mild but can be rainy, so pack appropriately.

- **Stay Hydrated:** The Mediterranean climate can be warm, especially in the summer months.

Always carry a water bottle with you and drink plenty of fluids.

With these practical tips, you'll be well-prepared to navigate Heraklion smoothly, ensuring a memorable and enjoyable visit to this vibrant city!

Sustainable Tourism

As travelers increasingly prioritize sustainability, Heraklion has taken significant steps toward promoting eco-friendly tourism. With its rich history, natural beauty, and vibrant culture, Heraklion offers many opportunities for responsible travel, allowing visitors to enjoy the island while minimizing their environmental impact. Here's a guide to sustainable tourism practices and eco-friendly activities in the region.

Eco-Friendly Activities in Heraklion

1. Hiking and Nature Trails

- **Why It's Sustainable:** Exploring Crete's natural landscapes by foot or bike is one of the best ways to minimize your environmental footprint. The island offers a wealth of hiking trails, many of which pass through protected areas and offer stunning views of the Mediterranean Sea and rugged mountains.

- **Top Trails to Explore:**

  ❖ **Gorge of Agioi Pantes:** A hike through a lush ravine that's perfect for nature lovers and birdwatchers.

  ❖ **Mount Youchtas:** Known for its Minoan archaeological site and panoramic views, this hike is ideal for combining history and nature.

❖ **Aposelemis River Trail:** A walk along the river, offering a tranquil environment and opportunities for wildlife spotting.

2. Eco-Friendly Beaches

- **Why It's Sustainable:** Many of Crete's beaches have earned Blue Flag status, which means they meet stringent environmental and safety standards. These beaches focus on clean water, waste management, and conservation efforts.

- **Top Eco-Conscious Beaches in Heraklion:**

  ❖ **Ammoudara Beach:** Known for its clean water and eco-friendly management, this beach is also a great spot for water sports.

  ❖ **Matala Beach:** A protected area with historical significance and clear, warm waters. Visitors are encouraged to respect the local wildlife and environment.

3. Botanical Gardens and Natural Reserves

- **Why It's Sustainable:** Many botanical gardens and reserves in Heraklion aim to preserve native plants and animal species. Visiting these places is a great way to learn about Crete's biodiversity while supporting conservation efforts.

- **Top Eco-Friendly Sites:**
  - **The Cretaquarium:** A responsible aquarium focused on marine life education and conservation.
  - **Heraklion's Botanical Park:** Located on the outskirts of the city, this park focuses on the preservation of Cretan plant life. It's a

great place for a relaxing walk while learning about local flora.

4. Organic Farming and Eco Tours

- **Why It's Sustainable:** Crete has a long history of agriculture, and many farmers are adopting organic and sustainable farming practices. Eco-tours offer a hands-on way to learn about organic farming, olive oil production, and sustainable viticulture.

- **Top Eco-Friendly Farm Tours:**
    - ❖ **Olive Oil Tours:** Many local olive farms offer tours where visitors can learn about the organic cultivation and harvesting process, as well as sample high-quality extra virgin olive oil.

- ❖ **Winery Tours:** Explore Cretan wineries that focus on sustainable, organic viticulture. Taste local wines while supporting eco-conscious producers.

- ❖ **Agritourism:** Participate in workshops on organic gardening, bread baking, or traditional cheese-making in rural Crete.

5. Eco-Friendly Boat Tours and Water Sports

- **Why It's Sustainable:** Many boat tours around Heraklion now emphasize sustainability, focusing on wildlife conservation and responsible marine tourism. These tours allow visitors to explore Crete's crystal-clear waters without negatively impacting the marine environment.

- **Eco-Friendly Activities:**

    ❖ **Eco Boat Tours:** Explore the stunning coastline on small, eco-friendly boats that minimize pollution and respect marine ecosystems.

    ❖ **Kayaking and Paddleboarding:** These low-impact activities allow you to enjoy the waters without disturbing the natural environment, perfect for peaceful exploration.

    ❖ **Snorkeling and Scuba Diving with Conservation Focus:** Choose dive operators who are committed to marine conservation, ensuring that underwater ecosystems are protected during your visit.

Responsible Travel Practices

1. Minimizing Waste

- **Why It's Important:** The growing number of tourists can contribute to waste accumulation, so it's essential to minimize your waste while visiting. Many areas in Heraklion now promote waste reduction and recycling, making it easier for visitors to do their part.

- **Responsible Practices:**

  - **Reusable Water Bottles:** Carry a reusable water bottle to avoid single-use plastic. Many restaurants and cafes offer refill stations for water.

  - **Zero-Waste Shopping:** Bring your own bags and avoid unnecessary packaging when shopping for souvenirs or local products.

- ❖ **Proper Waste Disposal:** Always dispose of waste in designated bins, and take extra care to recycle where possible.

2. Supporting Local and Sustainable Businesses

- **Why It's Important:** By supporting local, sustainable businesses, you contribute to the local economy and encourage the continued growth of environmentally conscious practices.

- **How to Support:**

  - ❖ **Shop Local:** Choose local markets and shops that sell handmade or organic products, such as artisanal pottery, organic wines, and locally grown produce.

- **Eat at Eco-Conscious Restaurants:** Opt for restaurants that focus on organic, locally sourced ingredients and sustainable practices. Many Cretan tavernas serve farm-to-table meals, which support local agriculture.

- **Choose Eco-Friendly Accommodations:** Stay in hotels or guesthouses that prioritize sustainability by using energy-efficient systems, water-saving measures, and eco-friendly products. Look for accommodations with certifications like Green Key or EarthCheck.

3. Respecting Local Culture and Traditions

- **Why It's Important:** Sustainable tourism is about preserving the cultural heritage of a destination as much as protecting the environment. Respecting local customs and traditions helps ensure that tourism benefits the community and doesn't disrupt its way of life.

- **How to Respect Local Culture:**

  - ❖ **Learn About Local Customs:** Before visiting religious or historical sites, take the time to learn about their significance and adhere to appropriate behavior.

  - ❖ **Respect Local Communities:** Be considerate of local lifestyles, particularly in rural areas where traditions and customs may differ from urban life.

  - ❖ **Participate in Cultural Workshops:** Many local artisans offer classes on traditional crafts such as pottery, weaving, and olive oil production. These workshops not only provide an authentic experience but also support local businesses.

4. Minimizing Carbon Footprint

- **Why It's Important:** Traveling to Crete can involve significant carbon emissions, especially when flying. By adopting sustainable practices during your stay, you can offset some of your environmental impact.

- **How to Minimize Your Carbon Footprint:**

  - **Public Transportation:** Use public buses or walk whenever possible instead of renting a car.

  - **Eco-Friendly Transfers:** If you need to use taxis, opt for electric or hybrid cars, which are increasingly available in Heraklion.

- ❖ **Offset Carbon Emissions:** Consider purchasing carbon offsets to compensate for the emissions associated with your flight.

Heraklion is embracing sustainable tourism by offering travelers plenty of opportunities to explore its natural beauty and rich culture while minimizing their environmental impact. By participating in eco-friendly activities and practicing responsible travel, visitors can contribute to the preservation of Crete's landscapes and traditions for generations to come.

Useful Resources

To make your visit to Heraklion more enjoyable and organized, here are some helpful resources you can rely on during your trip. From maps and guides to essential apps and local service contacts, these resources will assist you in navigating the city and making the most of your time in Crete.

Maps

1. Digital Maps and Online Resources

- **Google Maps:** The go-to navigation tool for walking, driving, or public transportation directions. Google Maps will help you get from one place to another in Heraklion, show real-time traffic data, and locate nearby amenities.

- **Komoot:** For hiking enthusiasts, Komoot offers detailed trail maps, routes, and information about nature walks and outdoor activities in Heraklion and Crete.

- **VisitHeraklion.com:** This official tourism website provides comprehensive guides, maps of the city, and downloadable resources for key attractions, transportation routes, and accommodation suggestions.

2. **Paper Maps and Guides**

- **Heraklion Tourist Map:** Widely available at the Heraklion Airport, ferry ports, and local tourist offices, these maps provide helpful details on city streets, transportation hubs, and points of interest.

Recommended Apps for Travelers

1. Travel & Transportation Apps

- **Ferryhopper:** If you're planning on taking ferries around Crete or the Greek islands, this app helps you book tickets and find routes. It covers all ferry services departing from Heraklion.

- **Moovit:** For using public transportation in Heraklion, Moovit gives real-time information on bus schedules, routes, and connections. It's helpful for exploring the city and surrounding areas using buses.

- **Uber/Bolt:** Rideshare apps like Bolt (which operates in Heraklion) provide an easy way to get around the city without needing to hail a traditional taxi. These services are typically reliable and come with set pricing.

2. Restaurant and Dining Apps

- **Tripadvisor:** Tripadvisor is invaluable for finding reviews and recommendations for restaurants, cafes, and attractions. It helps you make informed decisions about where to eat or visit in Heraklion.

- **TheFork:** This app offers reservations at top restaurants in Heraklion, often with discounts or special offers. It's a great tool to find local dining options in advance.

- **HappyCow:** For vegan and vegetarian options, HappyCow provides a list of plant-based dining venues in Heraklion, ranging from casual eateries to more upscale options.

3. Activity and Experience Apps

- **GetYourGuide:** This app lets you book guided tours, skip-the-line tickets for popular attractions like Knossos Palace, and day trips from Heraklion. It's perfect for organizing unique and customized experiences in the area.

- **Viator:** Viator offers similar booking services for tours and experiences. You can browse activities like private tours, archaeological visits, and even cooking classes or traditional music performances in Crete.

- **Komoot:** Ideal for outdoor activities like hiking, biking, and nature walks, Komoot helps you discover scenic trails and plan your routes in Heraklion's nature reserves and coastal areas.

4. Language & Translation Apps

- **Google Translate:** While many locals in Heraklion speak English, Google Translate is useful for communicating with those who prefer to speak Greek. The app can translate both text and voice, making it easier to navigate through menus, signs, and conversations.

- **Duolingo:** For those interested in learning some basic Greek phrases before their trip, Duolingo offers a fun and interactive way to get started with the Greek language.

Contact Information for Local Services

1. Tourist Information Centers

- **Heraklion Tourism Office:** Located near Lions Square in the city center, this is the go-to place for maps, brochures, and advice on attractions, accommodations, and local events.

- ❖ **Address:** 10-12 25th August Street, Heraklion
- ❖ **Phone:** +30 2810 246-856
- ❖ **Opening Hours:** Monday to Friday, 9:00 AM to 6:00 PM; Saturday, 9:00 AM to 2:00 PM

- **Heraklion Port Tourist Office:** This office at the ferry terminal offers brochures, maps, and advice for travelers arriving by boat.

- ❖ **Address:** Heraklion Port, Ferry Terminal
- ❖ **Phone:** +30 2810 343-951

2. Medical Services

- **Heraklion General Hospital:** The main hospital in the city, offering emergency services and general healthcare.

  - **Address:** 1 Vasilissis Sofias Avenue, Heraklion
  - **Phone:** +30 2813 400-500
  - **Emergency Services (24/7):** Dial 166

- **Pharmacies:** Pharmacies are abundant in Heraklion, and most open from 9:00 AM to 2:00 PM and then 5:30 PM to 8:30 PM. For emergencies, there is always a pharmacy open at night; check local signs for the nearest one.

  - **Emergency Pharmacy:** Check for the nearest pharmacy on duty at the time (often displayed at the entrance of local pharmacies).

3. Local Transportation

- **Heraklion Bus Station (KTEL):** The main bus station for intercity and regional travel. KTEL buses connect Heraklion to other towns on the island, including Rethymno, Chania, and Agios Nikolaos.

    ❖ **Address:** 2, 28th October Street, Heraklion

    ❖ **Phone:** +30 2810 240-109

    ❖ **Website:** www.kteheraklion.gr

- **Heraklion Taxi Service:** You can easily find taxis in Heraklion or book one via a phone call or taxi app. Many taxis accept ridesharing requests through apps like Bolt.

- ❖ **Taxi Stand (Central):** Lions Square, Heraklion

- ❖ **Phone (Taxi Dispatch):** +30 2810 221-100

4. Emergency Contacts

- **Police:** Dial 100 in case of any emergency.

- **Fire Department:** Dial 199 for fire-related emergencies.

- **Emergency Medical Services:** Dial 166 for an ambulance.

These resources are invaluable for ensuring a smooth and hassle-free experience in Heraklion. By making use of maps, apps, and important contact information, you'll be well-equipped to explore the city, manage your travel, and address any issues that may arise during your stay.

Conclusion

Making the Most of Your Heraklion Adventure

Heraklion, the vibrant capital of Crete, offers an incredible blend of ancient history, stunning natural landscapes, and modern attractions. Whether you're exploring the legendary Palace of Knossos, immersing yourself in the city's rich culture, relaxing on its beautiful beaches, or indulging in its gastronomic delights, there's something for everyone in this captivating destination. By following this guide, you can make the most of your time in Heraklion, ensuring that every moment of your trip is memorable and fulfilling.

As you embark on your adventure, take time to savor the local experiences that truly define Crete: the warmth of the locals, the flavors of traditional Cretan cuisine, and the breathtaking natural beauty that surrounds the city. Whether you're visiting for a short getaway or a longer exploration, Heraklion promises a travel experience that combines both ancient wonders and contemporary charm.

Final Travel Tips for Heraklion

1. Plan Ahead, But Be Flexible: While Heraklion offers a wide range of activities and attractions, the city can get crowded, especially during peak tourist seasons. Plan ahead for popular sites like the Palace of Knossos and Heraklion Archaeological Museum, but also leave room for spontaneity.

Some of the best experiences may come from wandering the historic streets of the old town or discovering hidden gems recommended by locals.

2. Don't Skip the Local Cuisine: Cretan food is renowned for its fresh, flavorful ingredients. From savory moussaka to delicate lamb dishes and sweet pastries like baklava, there's no shortage of delicious options to try. Be sure to visit local markets for fresh produce and consider a food tour to fully experience the culinary delights of the island.

3. Embrace the Outdoors: Heraklion's natural beauty is not to be missed. If you enjoy outdoor activities, make time for a hike or a boat tour. Whether it's hiking up Mount Youchtas, swimming in crystal-clear waters, or simply enjoying the sunset from a quiet beach, the outdoor adventures in Heraklion offer an escape into nature.

4. Respect Local Culture and Traditions: As with any travel destination, being respectful of local customs and traditions is crucial. Greek people are known for their hospitality, so a friendly approach and willingness to learn a few words of Greek (like "Kalimera" for good morning) will go a long way in making your experience even more enriching.

5. Travel Light and Stay Sustainable: Sustainability is key to preserving the beauty and culture of Heraklion. Pack smart by bringing reusable water bottles, eco-friendly toiletries, and comfortable shoes for exploring the city and its natural sites. Be mindful of waste and support local businesses that emphasize sustainable practices.

6. Stay Safe and Informed: While Heraklion is generally a safe city for tourists, it's always a good idea to be aware of your surroundings and keep your belongings secure. Make sure to have the local emergency numbers saved, and check out local tips on safety from the Heraklion Tourist Office.

7. Take Time to Explore Beyond the City: Heraklion is the perfect base for exploring the rest of Crete. Whether it's a day trip to nearby Rethymno, a visit to the Lassithi Plateau, or a boat ride to Spinalonga Island, there's much more to discover outside the city. Renting a car or using local transportation options can open up the island's rich heritage and stunning scenery.

8. Enjoy the Moment: Above all, take the time to simply enjoy the beauty of Heraklion. Don't rush through your trip—whether it's relaxing in a charming café in the old town or watching the waves crash against the shore, Heraklion is a place meant to be savored.

Heraklion is a city that blends ancient civilization with modern-day excitement, offering travelers a truly unique experience. With the knowledge and resources provided in this guide, you're ready to explore all that this fascinating city has to offer. From historical landmarks to scenic beaches, culinary adventures to cultural discoveries, Heraklion promises to be a highlight of any trip to Crete. Enjoy your adventure and make unforgettable memories in this beautiful Mediterranean destination!